125 Inspirational Quotes for Strong Women

Phil Collins

Dedication

Dedicated to the resilient spirits that grace these pages – the 125 strong women who have left an indelible mark on the world. Your strength, courage, and wisdom inspire us all to rise above challenges. May these quotes be a beacon, a celebration of your resilience, and a reminder that every woman possesses an unwavering power within.

Here's to the extraordinary strength that lies within every woman's story.

Introduction

It takes courage, no matter who you are, to follow your dreams, confront injustice, or hold fast to your beliefs—especially when faced with opposition or conflicting information.

Particularly women should be honored for their perseverance in standing up for themselves or taking on the role of self-champion during trying circumstances. We're here to celebrate and disseminate the top 125 motivational sayings for powerful women because of this.

At some point in their life, many women experience feeling constrained by the expectations or views of others, or overlooked because of gender stereotypes. That does not imply, nevertheless, that women have avoided these difficulties. Instead, women have increased their willpower and tenacity to achieve amazing things, sometimes even in the face of overwhelming obstacles.

To others, this resembles practicing to be the greatest contender in a certain sport. Others may see this as battling for legislative reform in order to improve the lot of random people. For yet others, it's about accepting difficult times and seasons in order to gain empowerment.

Women are strong and brave, despite the vast range of personal situations that they may encounter. These powerful women's statements are really inspiring, regardless of your present situation in life.

These 125 strong women quotes will encourage you whether you've always thought of strength as one of your best attributes or you're just getting started and have a more positive self-image!

125 Inspirational Quotes for Strong Women

1. "Ignore the glass ceiling and do your
work. If you're focusing on the glass
ceiling, focusing on what you don't have,
focusing on the limitations, then you will
be limited."
— Ava DuVernay

2. "There are two powers in the world;
one is the sword and the other is the pen.
There is a third power stronger than
both, that of women."
— Malala Yousafzai

3. "A woman is like a tea bag; you never know how strong it is until it's in hot water."
— **Eleanor Roosevelt**

4. "Life is very interesting... in the end, some of your greatest pains, become your greatest strengths."
— **Drew Barrymore**

5. "I had to remind myself of the truth of who I was and the reality that success wasn't defined by a result but by faithfulness. I had to remember that my identity and healing weren't dependent on the voices that surrounded me and that the truth wasn't dependent on popular opinion or cultural responses. I had to focus on what was real and true. The straight line instead of the crooked."
— **Rachael Denhollander**

6. "I can never be safe; I always try and go against the grain. As soon as I accomplish one thing, I just set a higher goal. That's how I've gotten to where I am."
— **Beyoncé**

7. "Optimism is the faith that leads to achievement. Nothing can be done without hope and confidence."
— Helen Keller

8. "I love hearing educated people speak and just shut everyone up. Knowledge is always the loudest voice."
— Zendaya

9. "Perhaps some detours aren't detours at all. Perhaps they are actually the path."
— **Katherine Wolf**

10. "Champions keep playing until they get it right."
— **Billie Jean King**

11. "Develop enough courage so that you can stand up for yourself and then stand up for somebody else."
— **Maya Angelou**

12. "I'd rather regret the risks that didn't work out than the chances I didn't take at all."
— **Simone Biles**

13. "The one person who will never leave us, whom we will never lose, is ourself. Learning to love our female selves is where our search for love must begin."
— **Bell Hooks**

14. "I don't want to be better than you or her or him - I want to be better than I am right now."
— **Kerri Walsh**

15. "If you don't see a clear path for what you want, sometimes you have to make it yourself."
— Mindy Kaling

16. "Work hard every day. No matter what your strengths and weaknesses, there's no substitute for hard work."
— Hope Solo

17. "I love challenging the status quo."
— **Sara Ramirez**

18. "I can if I want to because it's my
business."
— **Tabitha Brown**

19. "Be courageous. Challenge orthodoxy. Stand up for what you believe in. When you are in your rocking chair talking to your grandchildren many years from now, be sure you have a good story to tell."
— **Amal Clooney**

20. "True champions aren't always the ones that win, but those with the most guts."
— **Mia Hamm**

21. "Being a strong woman is very important to me. But doing it all on my own is not."
— **Reba McEntire**

22. "We might not be able to change our circumstances, but we CAN change our attitude."
— **Beth Moore**

23. " People have to go through things in order to become the person that they are today and that's that."
— **Sarah Hyland**

24. "I've always wanted to fight for people who didn't have arms. I've always wanted to speak up for people who don't have a voice. I've always wanted to protect people who couldn't protect themselves. It's my nature. It's my instinct."
— **Sophia Bush**

25. "I am learning every day to allow the space between where I am and where I want to be to inspire me and not terrify me."
— **Tracee Ellis Ross**

26. "We're here for a reason. I believe a bit of the reason is to throw little torches out to lead people through the dark."
— **Whoopi Goldberg**

27. "Because confidence is really trust in yourself, right? It has nothing to do with what someone else thinks of you; it's what you think of you."
— **Chrissy Metz**

28. "Change takes courage."
— **Alexandria Ocasio-Cortez**

29. "What if the things that have caused
the most hurt in your life became the
birthplaces of your deepest passions?"
— Jennie Allen

30. "A leader takes people where they
want to go. A great leader takes people
where they don't necessarily want to go,
but ought to be."
— Rosalynn Carter

31. "It's about putting in the hours and going through the paces."
— **Shawn Johnson**

32. "My best successes came on the heels of failures."
— **Barbara Corcoran**

33. "The question isn't who's going to let me; it's who is going to stop me."
— **Ayn Rand**

34. "Courage starts with showing up and letting ourselves be seen."
—**Brené Brown**

35. "If you are afraid of failure, you don't deserve success."
— **Nastia Liukin**

36. "If your actions create a legacy that inspires others to dream more, learn more, do more and become more, then, you are an excellent leader."
— **Dolly Parton**

37. "Hard days are the best because that's when champions are made."
— **Gabby Douglas**

38. "I don't believe in putting on airs. I call it like I see it."
— **Ellen Pompeo**

39. "Keep working even when no one is watching."
— **Alex Morgan**

40. "It takes courage and strength to be empathetic, and I'm very proudly an empathetic and compassionate leader. I am trying to chart a different path, and that will attract criticism but I can only be true to myself and the form of leadership I believe in."
— **Jacinda Ardern**

41. "I am no longer accepting the things I cannot change. I am changing the things I cannot accept."
— **Angela Davis**

42. "Joy is strength."
— **Mother Teresa**

43. "We still think of a powerful man as a born leader and a powerful woman as an anomaly."
— **Margaret Atwood**

44. "I really think a champion is defined not by their wins but by how they can recover when they fall."
— **Serena Williams**

45. "I believe in being strong when everything seems to be going wrong. I believe that happy girls are the prettiest girls. I believe that tomorrow is another day, and I believe in miracles."
— **Audrey Hepburn**

46. "The important thing is to always ask the world to do some things. But sometimes they cannot be done, so you have to take a stab, and you have to do them."
— **Malala Yousafzai**

47. "I am grateful for all those dark years,
even though in retrospect they seem like
a long, bitter prayer that was answered
finally."
— **Marilynne Robinson**

48. "If you overthink things, the moment
will pass you by."
— **Maya Moore**

49. "Find the smartest people you can
and surround yourself with them."
— **Marissa Meyer**

50. "I just want women to always feel in
control. Because we're capable, we're so
capable."
— **Nicki Minaj**

51. "You draw your own box. You introduce yourself as who you are. . . . You create the identity you want for yourself."
— **Meghan Markle**

52. "Anger is not inherently destructive. My anger can be a force for good. My anger can be creative and imaginative, seeing a better world that doesn't yet exist. It can fuel a righteous movement toward justice and freedom."
— **Austin Channing Brown**

53. "Love is not a weak, spineless emotion; it is a powerful moral force on the side of justice."
— **Bernice King**

54. "There is power in seeing a face that looks like yours do something, be someone. There is power in moving from the sidelines to the center."
— **Jenny Han**

55. "We need women who are so strong they can be gentle, so educated they can be humble, so fierce they can be compassionate, so passionate they can be rational, and so disciplined they can be free."
— **Kavita Ramdas**

56. "We may encounter many defeats but we must not be defeated."
— **Maya Angelou**

57. "I know my worth. I embrace my power. I say if I'm beautiful. I say if I'm strong. You will not determine my story. I will."
— **Amy Schumer**

58. "She is clothed with strength and dignity, and she laughs without fear of the future."
— **Proverbs 31:25**

59. "Life is either a daring adventure, or
nothing."
— **Helen Keller**

60. "Perseverance is failing 19 times and
succeeding the 20th."
— **Julie Andrews**

61. "Don't look at the big picture as the only achievement. Start with set, smart goals and work up to something bigger."
— **Jordyn Wieber**

62. "Some people say I have attitude - maybe I do... but I think you have to. You have to believe in yourself when no one else does - that makes you a winner right there."
— **Venus Williams**

63. "I encourage women to step up. Don't
wait for somebody to ask you."
— **Reese Witherspoon**

64. "You have to rely on your support
system. Growing up, I always thought it
was a sign of weakness to ask for help,
but now I realize it's really a sign of
strength to say, 'I need help, I can't do it
all.'"
— **Kerri Walsh**

65. "Sometimes the future changes quickly and completely, and we're left with only the choice of what to do next. We can choose to be afraid of it. Just stand there trembling, not moving. Assuming the worst that can happen. Or we step forward into the unknown, and assume it will be brilliant."
— **Sandra Oh**

66. "Don't settle for average. Bring your best to the moment. Then, whether it fails or succeeds, at least you know you gave all you had. We need to live the best that's in us."
— **Angela Bassett**

67. "Power isn't control at all—power is strength, and giving that strength to others. A leader isn't someone who forces others to make him stronger; a leader is someone willing to give his strength to others that they may have the strength to stand on their own."
— Beth Revis

68. "Learn to embrace your own unique beauty, celebrate your unique gifts with confidence. Your imperfections are actually a gift."
— Kerry Washington

69. "There's nothing wrong with a woman being comfortable, confident."
— **Selena Gomez**

70. "Be bold, be courageous, be your best."
— **Gabrielle Giffords**

71. "Just remember, you can do anything you set your mind to, but it takes action, perseverance, and facing your fears."
— **Gillian Anderson**

72. "If we cultivate compassion for those who have hurt us, we have the possibility of overcoming our anger, pain, and fear. Compassion is a great medicine."
— **Goldie Hawn**

73. "If you set out to be liked, you would be prepared to compromise on anything at any time, and you would achieve nothing."
— **Margaret Thatcher**

74. "Anyone can hide. Facing up to things, working through them, that's what makes you strong."
— **Sarah Dessen**

75. "Courage, sacrifice, determination, commitment, toughness, heart, talent, guts. That's what little girls are made of; the heck with sugar and spice."
— Bethany Hamilton

76. "Enjoy life, study hard, play hard, be kind to other people, set high standards, and don't be afraid to say 'No.'"
— Nia Long

77. "Instead of looking at the past, I put myself ahead twenty years and try to look at what I need to do now in order to get there then."
— **Diana Ross**

78. "You can't always control the circumstances - only how you react to those circumstances; you can always control your attitude and your effort."
— **Jennie Finch**

79. "I don't go by the rule book. I lead from the heart, not the head."
—Diana Spencer, Princess of Wales

80. "Never doubt that a small group of thoughtful committed citizens can change the world. Indeed, it is the only thing that ever has."
— Margaret Mead

81. "I would like to instill in people just to
work hard. As long as they keep at it,
their dreams will happen."
— **Misty May-Treanor**

82. "I alone cannot change the world, but
I can cast a stone across the water to
create many ripples."
— **Mother Teresa**

83. "I have always been one to encourage perseverance."
— **Christina Aguilera**

84. "I've had to learn through experiences not to be afraid to fail. You don't know what the future holds for you. You can hope your dreams come true, but you have to be fearless. I don't want to look back and think, 'What if?'"
— **Nastia Liukin**

85. "I don't have any time to stay up all night worrying about what someone who doesn't love me has to say about me."
— **Viola Davis**

86. "I don't need easy, I just need possible."
— **Bethany Hamilton**

87. "You can waste your lives drawing lines. Or you can live your life crossing them."
— **Shonda Rhimes**

88. "I'm trying to take the stigma off the word [ambitious] so we encourage more little girls to be ambitious, because I do think that's how society will change."
— **Reese Witherspoon**

89. "Sports provide girls with the opportunity to develop a better relationship with their bodies. They can be aggressive on the court, be strong and still be feminine."
— **Gabrielle Reece**

90. "I have a strong personality, and I say what I think."
— **Penelope Cruz**

91. "Always be a first-rate version of yourself, instead of a second-rate version of somebody else."
— **Judy Garland**

92. "I didn't have anybody. Really, no foundation in life, so I had to make my own way. Always, from the start. I had to go out in the world and become strong, to discover my mission in life."
— **Tina Turner**

93. "When you fail you learn from the mistakes you made and it motivates you to work even harder."
— **Natalie Gulbis**

94. "Our happiness is certainly mixed in with the tragedies of life. You have to find the lemonade. You have to find the silver lining in the middle of everything that happens in life."
— **Chandra Wilson**

95. "When my body is strong, I feel stronger inside. I feel more capable of handling emotional situations."
— **Mariska Hargitay**

96. "Both men and women should feel free to be sensitive. Both men and women should feel free to be strong."
— **Emma Watson**

97. "Don't waste your energy trying to change opinions... Do your thing and don't care if they like it."
— **Tina Fey**

98. "We must reject not only the stereotypes that others hold of us, but also the stereotypes that we hold of ourselves."
— **Shirley Chisholm**

99. "I would encourage you to set really high goals. Set goals that, when you set them, you think they're impossible. But then every day you can work towards them, and anything is possible, so keep working hard and follow your dreams."
— Katie Ledecky

100. "Doubt is a killer. You just have to know who you are and what you stand for."
— Jennifer Lopez

101. "The majority of the things that I do, I'm actually afraid to do, but you just have to have a positive attitude and block out any fears that you have."
— **Aly Raisman**

102. "Fill your life with women that empower you, that help you believe in your magic and aid them to believe in their own exceptional power and their incredible magic too. Women that believe in each other can survive anything. Women who believe in each other create armies that will win kingdoms and wars."
— **Nikita Gill**

103. "Think like a queen. A queen is not afraid to fail. Failure is another stepping stone to greatness."
— **Oprah Winfrey**

104. "Nothing I accept about myself can be used against me to diminish me."
— **Audre Lorde**

105. "I just love bossy women. I could be around them all day. To me, bossy is not a pejorative term at all. It means somebody's passionate and engaged and ambitious and doesn't mind learning."
— **Amy Poehler**

106. "Courage doesn't always roar, sometimes it's the quiet voice at the end of the day whispering I will try again tomorrow."
— **Mary Anne Radmacher**

107. "Above all, be the heroine of your life, not the victim."
— **Nora Ephron**

108. "Stay strong. Stand up. Have a voice."
— **Shawn Johnson**

109. "I think scars are like battle wounds – beautiful, in a way. They show what you've been through and how strong you are for coming out of it."
— **Demi Lovato**

110. "Celebrate what you've accomplished, but raise the bar a little higher each time you succeed."
— **Mia Hamm**

111. "You gain strength, courage, and confidence by every experience in which you really stop to look fear in the face. You are able to say to yourself, 'I lived through this horror. I can take the next thing that comes along.' You must do the thing you think you cannot do."
— **Eleanor Roosevelt**

112. "You may not always have a comfortable life and you will not always be able to solve all of the world's problems at once but don't ever underestimate the importance you can have because history has shown us that courage can be contagious and hope can take on a life of its own."
— **Michelle Obama**

113. "I believe in strong women. I believe
in the woman who is able to stand up for
herself. I believe in the woman who
doesn't need to hide behind her
husband's back. I believe that if you have
problems, as a woman you deal with
them, you don't play victim, you don't
make yourself look pitiful, you don't
point fingers. You stand and you deal.
You face the world with a head held high
and you carry the universe in your heart."
— C. JoyBell C.

114. "You can fall, but you can rise also."
— Angélique Kidjo

115. "Be strong, believe in who you are;
be strong, believe in what you feel."
— **Melissa Etheridge**

116. "Life is not easy for any of us. But
what of that? We must have perseverance
and, above all, confidence in ourselves.
We must believe we are gifted for
something and that this thing must be
attained."
— **Marie Curie**

117. "I love argument, I love debate. I don't expect anyone just to sit there and agree with me, that's not their job."
— **Margaret Thatcher**

118. "You need to learn how to select your thoughts just the same way you select your clothes every day. This is a power you can cultivate. If you want to control things in your life so bad, work on the mind. That's the only thing you should be trying to control."
— **Elizabeth Gilbert**

119. "I have chosen to no longer be apologetic for my femaleness and my femininity. And I want to be respected in all of my femaleness because I deserve to be."
— **Chimamanda Ngozi Adichie**

120. "But the real secret to total gorgeousness is to believe in yourself, have self-confidence, and try to be secure in your decisions and thoughts."
— **Kirsten Dunst**

121. "Strong women don't play the victim.
Don't make themselves look pitiful and
don't point fingers. They stand and they
deal."
— **Mandy Hale**

122. "Women who had the strength to
really stand up for something that they
knew needed to be done is the best
example of no matter how small you
might feel, how low you may feel on the
ladder or the totem pole, no matter what
color you are, no matter what gender you
are, you have a voice and you certainly
have the right to speak up for what is
right."
— **Meghan Markle**

123. "My mother told me to be a lady. And for her, that meant be your own person, be independent."
— **Ruth Bader Ginsburg**

124. "A true diva is graceful, and talented, and strong, and fearless and brave and someone with humility."
— **Beyoncé**

125. "A really strong woman accepts the war she went through and is ennobled by her scars."
— **Carly Simon**

Closing Remark

In conclusion, may the echoes of these powerful voices linger, reminding us of the strength, resilience, and wisdom that define the essence of womanhood.

Let these words be a source of inspiration and empowerment, propelling us forward with the collective force of 125 strong women.

May their stories continue to shape our narratives and inspire greatness in each of us.

Here's to the enduring strength that unites us all.